I0420890

'WIGGLE'

THE LONG RED WORM

Nester Kadzviti Murira

0

© N. Murira (2015)

All rights reserved

UNDER THE DOOR MAT

Every morning after cleaning her little house spotless clean, Grandma cleans her door step with a rough broom.

Brush! Brush! Brush! She cleans her door mat.

She sweeps away a few leaves that drop off from the big tall tree in her garden.

She lifts the door mat and shakes

it clean of mud and dust.

Shake! Shake! Shake!

She shakes the door mat and

slaps it on the broom handle.

Whack, whack, whack! Boom!

Boom! Boom!

All the leaves fall. All the dust flies

away!

One morning, grandma lifted the

mat and saw a wiggling worm.

"Tanaka, come and see this long,

thin, red worm!" Grandma called.

The long, thin, red worm wiggled backwards to the crack on the door step.

"Grandma, where is he going?" Tanaka asked.

"I wonder," said Grandma. "Let us watch him".

The worm wiggled to the crack in the stoop and lay over the crack. He let his body slide into the crack slowly. In a short while he was gone!

"AH! Clever worm! He is gone!"
Grandma said with a little smile on
her face.

"He has run away, grandma.
Maybe he has gone back to his
mother. Maybe he was lost."
Tanaka said looking at the crack in
the stoop.

"Well, he may come to visit us
again,Tanaka." Grandma said.
"Let's look out for him."

The next morning, grandma lifted the mat as she cleaned. There was the long thin red worm again!

"Tanaka, the worm is here again!" Grandma called. Tanaka rushed to the door. He and his Grandma watched the worm wiggle to the crack in the stoop.

"Look, Grandma, he is hurrying away again!" Tanaka whispered excitedly his eyes wide open and fixed on the worm.

One moment the worm was over

the crack, the next minute he was

gone!

"Look, grandma, he is gone

again!" Tanaka said surprised.

"Grandma, I am going to call him

Wiggle. He wiggles away into the

stoop all the time but, he likes

visiting us, grandma." Tanaka said.

"Oh, Wiggle! What a clever name

for our wiggling visitor, Tanaka!"

Grandma smiled at Tanaka.

WIGGLE VISITS TANAKA EVERY DAY

Every morning Tanaka waited for grandma to lift the door mat. Tanaka and his Grandma looked out for the thin, long, red worm, Wiggle.

Wiggle was under the mat every day. He wiggled down the crack in the stoop every time grandma lifted the door mat.

"So this is your home wise worm?" John asked leaning forward to watch Wiggle go to his hiding place.

"Why does Wiggle run away, grandma?"Tanaka asked his grandma.

"Wiggle feels warm under the mat." Grandma said. "When the mat is lifted, wiggle feels cold. He wiggles and hurries into the crack where it is warm."

"Why does he ever come out of the crack, grandma?" Tanaka asked.

"Wiggle is very happy under a wet mat. He can drink the water dripping from the mat. He stays cool under the mat."

'I think Wiggle likes us, Grandma." Tanaka said looking at their morning visitor.

'We can be friends, Wiggle. You are safe with us here.' Tanaka said.

Grandma smiled at Tanaka.

'Can I give him water, Grandma?'Tanaka asked.

'He got his water under the mat, Tanaka. Worms don't drink a lot of water. He won't drink it.' Grandma said smiling.

He must eat something, Grandma. I have not seen him eat anything.'

Tanaka looked at his Grandma.

'He eats when he goes down the crack, Tanaka. We can't see what

he does under the crack.'

Grandma said to Tanaka

WIGGLE GROWS BIG

"Look, Grandma, Wiggle is growing fatter and fatter every day. Soon he will be too big for the crack. Look he can hardly fit in the crack now." Tanaka pointed at the worm squeezing through the crack one morning.

'Wiggle eats his food well. He drinks a lot of water too. When you eat well and drink your glass of milk as I tell you always, you will grow to be a big strong boy." Grandma said.

"Grandma, where will Wiggle hide in winter? You said he does not like to be cold?"

"It is too cold under the mat in winter. Wiggle goes deep in the mud in the garden when winter comes." Grandma said.

"Where will you hide in the hot season, Wiggle? It is too hot and dry under the mat. There is no water to keep you cool under the mat. There is dust under the mat too. It is too hot and dry behind the stoop." Tanaka said looking at the big long fat red worm.

"Wiggle will stay deep in the soil where it is cool. He will hide away from the birds and the big black ants." Grandma said.

"I will miss you Wiggle. Grandma will miss you too. Won't you grandma?" Tanaka asked looking up at his grandma. Grandma smiled and nodded back at Tanaka.

WIGGLE GOES MISSING

One day, Wiggle was not under the mat in the morning.

Grandma and Tanaka looked at each other.

"Grandma, I think Wiggle found his mother. Maybe he was lost. Maybe he is not well." Tanaka said looking into the stoop crack with his eyes full of tears.

"Maybe he is too big to squeeze through the crack, Tanaka." Grandma said.

"Is Wiggle coming back when the rains come? Please come back when the cold and wind are gone. Wiggle, come back. We will wait for you." Tanaka said sadly as he looked down the crack where Wiggle had always wiggled into.

"Grandma, when does Wiggle come back? I miss him already." Tanaka said.

"We have to wait until the harsh winter goes away, Tanaka, then we can look around for Wiggle once more." Grandma put her hand on Tanaka's shoulder.

"Wiggle must be happy and warm in the mud in the garden. Maybe we will see him in the garden in summer. He will have grown too fat to wiggle out that tiny crack." Grandma told Tanaka.

www.ingramcontent.com/pod-product-compliance
Lightning Source LLC
Chambersburg PA
CBHW072025290526
45787CB00014B/1881